Directed Paths

Stories of God's Providences in My Life and That of My Family

Myrtle A. Neufeld.

by Myrtle Blabey Neufeld

2nd Revised Edition, 2005

All scripture quotations are from the King James
Version.

All names marked with an asterisk (*) are
pseudonyms.

Cover Design by PhotoMD (www.photomd.net)

ISBN: 1-893729-22-2
January, 2005

Acknowledgements

I would like to express my appreciation for, and say 'thank you,' first, to God for giving the abilities; then to Mrs. Mavis Oliver for the many hours she spent in editing the manuscript; to my children: Henry (who published this book), Patty, Robert, and Betty Rae, who have made the way so pleasant; and to my husband, Ray, who since 1946, has walked with me and strengthened me in the "directed paths."

Forward

by Henry E. Neufeld

A couple of years ago I began looking for prayer experiences to use in teaching. I wanted experiences that would awaken in my students a desire to live a life of prayer—modern stories that show how God still works in the lives of His servants.

It occurred to me that my parents had lived through just that kind of experiences. I asked my mother to tell some of these on tape. Later, we also got them in writing. The result is this booklet.

"Directed Paths" is part of the *Participatory Study Series* because it tells about participation in God's plan and God's action. In other books and pamphlets from the series you can read about how to pray, how to bring prayer groups together, and about people in the Bible who prayed and had their prayers answered. In this booklet of true stories from the 20th century, you are challenged to bring those prayer experiences alive for the here and now.

It is tempting to call my parents exceptional people, but I don't think it is a description with which they would be comfortable. They are simply servants of God, living a life under His guidance, and praying their way by faith step by step. This is a challenge for each of us. Whether we have given our life in service to people in other lands, or simply given ourselves to God as a witness to our immediate neighbors, these stories tell how God can work in our lives. They tell how God can use us in His service if we listen to Him and are obedient, regardless of how much or how little talent and education we have.

We live in a world of denominational barriers. My parents served as missionaries for the Seventh-day Adventist Church. You will find references in these stories to Sabbath School rather than Sunday School, to the search for a nearby Seventh-day Adventist Church, and to the work and writings of Ellen G. White. It is my prayer that you will not overlook these things, but will rather see God working through the lives of this Christian couple who are members of the Seventh-day Adventist Church.

I would like to conclude this introduction with the words of Ellen G. White; words I believe are exemplified in my parents' lives, and which I believe every Christian can take to heart:

Consecrate yourself to God in the morning; make this your very first work. Let your prayer be, "Take me, O Lord, as wholly Thine. I lay all my plans at Thy feet. Use me today in Thy service. Abide with me, and let all my work be wrought in Thee."

— Steps to Christ, p. 70

If each of us did this daily, imagine what God could do with us!

Henry E. Neufeld
Pensacola, FL
April 22, 1999

Introduction
God Who Made the Sun to Rise

If we have forgotten the name of our God, or stretched out our hands to a strange god; shall not God search this out? For he knoweth the secrets of the heart.

Psalm 44:20-21

We have a loving heavenly Father. I used to think of Him as a tyrant bent on destroying us and only the begging of our precious Savior, Jesus, kept Him from it. Imagine my joy the day Jesus' words, "The Father Himself loveth you" became real for me! With this, other scriptures began flashing through my mind. "God so loved the world, that he gave his only begotten son, that whosoever believeth in him should not perish, but have everlasting life. For God sent not his Son into the world to condemn the world; but that the world through him might be saved." (John 3:16-17) This comes from a Father who asks us to trust Him and has promised to direct our paths.

I was twenty years old before I realized that God really was directing my paths. During a particularly difficult trial, I prayed for guidance. Opening my Bible, my eyes fell on "trust in the Lord with all thine heart; and lean not unto thine own understanding.

1

In all thy ways acknowledge him, and he shall direct thy paths." (Proverbs 3:5-6). For over sixty years, I have claimed that promise as my life theme.

However, there is also a false god who brought sin upon this earth. His name is Satan and he wants to take God's place and lead us astray. How can I be sure I am not praying to this false god who is able to transform himself into an angel of light? A simple story will illustrate.

A heathen family of four; father, mother, and two little girls, lived near a mission station in India. They never went to the station because they feared the missionaries. They were a very poor family, and the time came when their need was so great that the parents decided to sell their daughters as slaves in the temple. One morning the father began the trip to the temple with his two little girls. The mother stayed home and prayed. She had been praying for a long time. Not to her heathen gods, but to the God who made the sun to rise! She prayed every morning when she went down to the river at sunrise to get water for the day. Though the family were sun worshippers, she did not pray to the sun. Surely it could not rise by itself! She decided there must be a God who made it rise, and she prayed to that God.

With a heavy heart on the day she watched her small daughters go away, she prayed, "O God, who makes the sun come up in the morning, please take care of my little girls. You know we don't want them to be sold."

The Lord was not unmindful of her prayers. While on his way, the father noticed that the path to the temple led right through the mission compound. He was frightened and wondered what he should do. With no other way to go, he quietly continued his journey watching for danger. At that very time the missionary was out for an early morning stroll and met them.

He asked the father, "Where are you going, my friend?"

Anxiously, the father answered, "I am going to the temple to sell my two girls for we are very much in need of money."

The kindness of the missionary began to melt the father's fear. "Will you sell them to me?" asked the missionary. He named a price and said, "We will be good to them, feed them, and teach them to read and write."

The father hesitated. The missionary was kind. The money offer was much more than he would get at the temple. Also, with the girls close by, maybe he and his wife would be able to see them once in a while.

The God who directs paths and makes the sun to rise in the morning spoke to that father's mind and he said, "Yes, I will sell them to you."

The little girls were sad to see their father leave, but they were treated so kindly by the missionaries that they soon began to love their new home. The parents were encouraged to visit the mission and eventually, they all learned of Jesus and were baptized. The mother was happy to learn about the God who makes the sun come up in the morning.

Was not this a good test of the true God, the God who directs paths and makes the sun to rise, the God who made all things - the earth and sky, the sea and the fountains of water, and all things that are in them?

It is my desire that the stories I share on how God has directed my paths will give Him glory and point others to Him. I firmly believe that we need not fear the future when we remember what God has done for us in the past. Psalm 143:5 says, *"I remember the days of old; I meditate on all thy works; I muse on the work of thy hands."* Let us think of our minds as having walls where memory pictures hang. With the mind's eye, we can view them frequently. We can take down the ugly ones and forget the bad experiences while we keep our minds fixed upon our heavenly Father's love. Let us also remember that when we are prone to wander away from God, He has a promise for us in Psalm 44:20-21. *"If we have forgotten the name of our God, or stretched out our hands to a strange god; shall not God search this out? For he knoweth the secrets of the heart."*

God does search it out. He lets us know, and draws us back to Him - the one who made the sun to rise, the true God. Therefore, let us direct our prayers to Him. My mother taught me from the Scriptures that we are to pray to the Father in the Son's name. This means we are to address the Father first then pray in Jesus' name or for His sake, and allow Him to direct our paths.

Chapter 1
Background Information
Home Influences

Cast thy bread upon the waters; for thou shalt find it after many days.

Ecclesiastes 11:1

My stories may be better understood through a preview of some conditions under which I was raised. My home was eleven miles from the small town of Dauphin in Manitoba, Canada. My father, Luke Blabey, a farmer and blacksmith, had homesteaded the place before he met and married my mother, Martha Ann Giles. My parents had a short courtship.

One day a minister came to Dauphin to hold evangelistic meetings. There was no music for the services. Someone told him about my father, a bachelor who played the violin. The minister went out to the farm and asked my father to come in each evening and play for the services. Also, the minister heard about a young lady, my mother, who could play the pump organ. She lived in the south part of Manitoba in Altamont. He wrote and invited her to come play the organ. For six weeks the young couple sang and played together for the services. They fell in love and asked the minister to marry them before he left. It might be a long time before another minister would come to town.

I was born on that Manitoba farm, May 28, 1918, one of eleven children born to my parents. I am thankful to have grown up on the farm and to have had my Christian Seventh-day Adventist parents. I consider this to be the first providence of my life.

My earliest childhood memory is of an event that occurred when I was three years old. For several years after World War I, a flu epidemic swept across the land and seemed to rage for some time each year. In 1921, everyone in my family became ill with this flu except myself, my four-year-old sister, Alma, and Wilfred the hired man. Wilfred kept up the farm chores and now had the added responsibility of cooking and caring for the family. With all other family members confined to their beds, it became the duty of Alma and me to help Wilfred. I remember distinctly how we helped. Wilfred prepared the food, served it on the plates then told us where to take it. We would take turns going up the stairs with these plates of food. For two little girls, who ordinarily climbed the stairs only by holding onto the rail, this became a task. We would place the plate on a step above as far as we could reach, climb to it, move the plate again, etc. until we reached the top. After everyone was fed, we had to take the plates back down to Wilfred. Not recognizing the seriousness of the situation, at night, when we were in bed, we would groan as we had heard the rest do, then laugh at ourselves.

Travel was not easy in those days. The trip to town by horse took three or more hours. Cars were such rarity that whenever we heard one coming, we ran out to watch it go by. Besides, cars were not too useful. During the winter, with no snowploughs (not yet invented) or salt (unheard of for roads), it was not possible to move all the mounds of snow from the unpaved roads. The later advent of a few snowmobiles in the community was a great blessing. Even in the summer months, travel was difficult, especially after a rain. It was easy for cars to get stuck in the muddy roads.

For many years, we did not have washing machines. The clothes were washed with an old scrub board and hung outside on a line to dry. We relished the sweet, fresh outdoor scent. In the winter, the clothes had to be brought in a few at a time and dried around the stove. It was not unusual for the temperature to drop to 40 and more degrees below zero and it could take as long as three days to wash and dry sheets. This helps to explain the story of why my mother took sheets from the bed to make a much needed layette without first washing them.

I do not know when a hospital was first built in our town. All our neighbors lived ten or more miles from town. No one went to the doctor unless it was serious. My mother was the neighborhood nurse. She had no training but seemed to know what to do. She used simple remedies and the Lord blessed her efforts. Her nursing skills included delivering babies, nursing people through flu, quinsy (abscess on tissue around the tonsils) and other diseases. We children were not left out. She nursed us through scarlet fever, measles, chicken pox, whooping cough, whatever.   Only when the illness was beyond her abilities, were people sent to a doctor. Many times the doctor came out to the homes.   Death was common from childhood diseases, especially smallpox and diphtheria, since there were no preventive shots.   Two of my siblings died from whooping cough.

Iodine for cuts and sores was a favorite for my mother in preventing infection. I still recall the sting of it. It seemed to be a belief that if it did not hurt or taste bitter, a medicine was thought of no value. Iodine really worked, not only in the sting, but also in the remedy.   One day my younger brother, Ray stepped on a nail in the chicken yard and it went through his foot. My composed mother seemed in no hurry to pull out the nail.   She went to the chicken house and got a long, clean feather from a hen on the nest. Saturating the feather with iodine, she began to pull the nail out as I watched in wide-eye anticipation.   As she pulled the nail from the bottom of the foot, she pushed the iodine soaked feather into the hole from the top. The result was a disinfected wound that healed quickly.

Sometimes my mother would be gone for overnight or longer, and we children would take charge at home. We worked hard and Papa willingly accepted our efforts with the cooking and farm work. Even though we were very poor, my parents would make a sacrifice to give to those in greater need. However, it seemed we never lacked, and I remember Mama singing as she worked, "Cast your bread upon the waters, ye who have but scant supply". I do not remember any more except the ending, "and it will come back to you." Later, I realized this hymn came from Ecclesiastes 11:1.

My mother never accepted pay for her services. To her, it was a privilege. Before she and my father were married, she had planned to be a missionary nurse. However, with marriage her mission field became her large family and the neighborhood, but her dream was fulfilled through her children. Three of her daughters became nurses, two of whom were missionaries.

The nearest Seventh-day Adventist Church was a hundred miles away so we held home Sabbath School. Mama taught the lesson, gave a mission story and we sang hymns. Afterward, inspired from the service, we younger children would go out, climb up on the wagon and sing those hymns over and over. The two I remember most are "When the Roll is Called up Yonder, I'll Be There" and "Shall We Gather at the River."

Chapter 2

Providential Experiences
Childhood to Marriage

The Bolt That Held Me Fast

For he shall give his angels charge over thee, to keep thee in all thy ways.

Psalm 91:11

I have a small bump on my forehead. It is barely noticeable, but can be felt. For many years I thought it was a birthmark. Then one day my brother, Stan, who is four years older than I, told me this story about what happened to me when he was five. I was just learning to walk and very unsteady on my feet. It was winter with a roaring fire in the homemade barrel stove that Papa had made in his blacksmith shop. There were bolts sticking out. Toddling across the floor, I tripped and literally flew toward the hot stove. Angels were near because I did not get my entire forehead burned. Instead, the top of my forehead hit a hot bolt that entered the skin, burning partly into the bone. Papa caught me and turned me round and round to "unscrew" me from the bolt. Everyone was crying but rejoiced that I was alive.

Saved from Wild Horses

Some trust in chariots, and some in horses: but we will remember the name of the Lord our God.

Psalm 20:7

A man named Mr. Boyd had several beautiful horses that ran wild along the roadway and in vacant fields. We were told that they were harmless, but we children kept our distance when we walked the two and half miles to and from school. With several choices available, we were able to choose our route around the horses. One day we wanted to walk across a vacant field. The horses were in a corner about a half-mile away. We decided to take our chances. On this particular day, there were five of us - my ten year old brother, Stan; seven year old Alma, myself and two neighbor children, Lloyd age 7 and Meta, 6. We were almost across when we heard thundering hoofs.

"Run! Run! Boyd's horses are chasing us," Stan screamed.

We all began to run, but I never could run very fast. With dismay I saw the others crawling under the barbed wire fence to safety. I heard the thunder of hoofs closing in and knew I could not make it. I did not even think to pray, but the Lord says in Isaiah 65:24, *"And it shall come to pass, that before they call, I will answer, and while they are yet speaking, I will hear."* Even though I did not know

13

that verse at the time, the Lord knew. Suddenly I felt myself falling. I landed in soft, damp dirt and listened to the sound of hoofs as the horses turned and galloped away. I found myself in a pit and began to cry, sure the rest had run home and left me. Then I looked up and saw the anxious face of my brother looking down at me.

"We'll get you out," he said. Stan reached for one hand and Lloyd the other. With Alma and Meta holding onto them they pulled with all their might until I was out. When we got home and told Mama and Papa, neither of them knew of a pit being in that field.

But I know my angel was caring for me and that there **was** a pit in that field, because **I fell into it** and was saved from the wild horses!

Saved from Drowning

When thou passest through the waters, I will be with thee; and through the rivers, they shall not overflow thee...

Isaiah 43:2

In the winter, our river would freeze over with twelve to eighteen inches of ice. When spring came and the mountain snows melted, the ice would begin to thaw and break into large four to five foot chunks. The cracking, thundering roar when the ice broke could be heard for miles. We would run to watch the huge chunks pile up, break loose, swirl and plunge in their struggle to flow down the flooding river. It was a wonderful sight, but in the process the moving chunks dug large holes along the river bottom. Each year the holes were in different places. When it became warm enough for swimming, we used long sticks to find the deeper holes. We dared not take a chance in getting in over our heads.

Near the school, there was an ideal swimming spot underneath a bridge. Occasionally we were allowed to stay after school for a swim. One afternoon at the beginning of the season, we ran to the bridge and had a great time swimming. I became tired and decided to rest. When I lowered my feet, there was nothing underneath. The next thing I knew, I was lying on the shore and my schoolmates were about me, crying, "You were drowning but Betty pulled you out."

In my struggle, I had tried to pull her under, but thank the Lord He saved us both. We had not thought to measure the water that year because the place had always been just right.

The Swing

The eternal God is thy refuge, and underneath are the everlasting arms...

Deuteronomy 33:27

Lily and I were the best of friends. Because we lived so far apart, we did everything together at school. Sometimes we got into trouble. Mama had a rule that we must come home immediately after school to do our chores. Once I got a worthwhile whipping because I had a difficult time keeping this rule. One night before that punishment, Lily and I decided to stop by the swing near our school. The swing was a board hung about one and a half feet from the ground with eight-foot side ropes strung between two tall trees. Two children could have a good swing by standing on the board and taking turns pumping to make the swing go higher and higher.

We stopped for just one swing, but were having so much fun we forgot about the time. Suddenly, on one of our up-swings, the rope broke and sent us hurling through the air. We landed in a nearby ditch filled with dried tree branches with me on top of Lily. At first, we were shocked and anxious about staying so long. Then we noticed blood on Lily's leg and saw a large hole where the flesh had been gouged out. Frightened, we began struggling to get Lily home.

Fortunately her house was near the school. By the time we got her home, Lily was in much pain. Her dad sent me to the nearest neighbor's house about a half mile away for iodine. Trembling with fright, I ran all the way.

In this age of medical care, Lily would have been back to school in a few days, but back then she missed two months while her leg healed. We were sorry for our disobedience and grateful that we had not been killed because of it. I was also grateful for Mama's understanding. Surely she represented our God who bears long with the children of men.

Born Again

But I will sacrifice unto thee with the voice of thanksgiving; I will pay that that I have vowed. Salvation is of the Lord.

Jonah 2:9

My parents taught us great Christian principles. They taught us to work hard, to be honest, faithful and to go the second mile. Even though they set the Christian example, we had to accept Christ on our own.

As a child, I loved to read, but I did not always choose my books from the school library wisely. I loved fairy stories. I now believe them to be a tool of Satan because it was difficult for me to relate to angels in a real way. The angels seemed like the fairies to me. I am sure this is Satan's plan - to counterfeit the angels so children will not have the reality. Mama tried to direct me toward better reading materials, but never forced me. She often referred me to some books at home by saying, "Why don't you read this?"

One day when I was thirteen years old and Mama was away, I finished my chores and, with nothing else to read, picked up one of Mama's little books. I became so engrossed that I could not put it down. Right then and there, I gave my heart to Jesus and experienced my first conversion. The book, "Early

Writings" was written by Mrs. E.G. White about her Christian experiences. It was thrilling. I was happy when a minister could come to baptize me.

I said my first conversion because I believe what John Wesley said when someone asked him why he preached so much on why you must be born again. He answered, "Because ye must be born again, and again, and again." It means a daily conversion.

I was so happy in my new experience. When I hunted cows in the pasture and woods, I would lift my voice in songs of praise. I found a place hidden from view and made my Bethel. There I would kneel to pray. Then I would sing. One thing that made this little corner so lovely was a six-inch high spruce tree. We didn't see those in our woods. They were eighteen miles away in the mountains. I think the Lord gave that little tree especially to me.

Shortly after my conversion, the Lord gave me a beautiful dream. I dreamed I saw Jesus coming in the clouds of heaven. He was so lovely. His face was so kind, and the angels surrounding Him were very beautiful. As they hovered in the sky, a sentence, the letters of which were formed with stars, moved across the sky above the heads of the angels. It read, "Salvation is of the Lord". All the words of the sentence moved together. I woke up and rejoiced over what I had dreamed. Years later, I found these words in Jonah 2:9.

Chapter 3

Mama and Papa, the Good Samaritans

He answereth and saith unto them, He that hath two coats, let him impart to him that hath none; and he that hath meat, let him do likewise.

Luke 3:11

It was wintertime and very cold. Sleigh bells could be heard on the frosty air for a long way down the road. We loved to guess what neighbor was coming by the sound of the bells. Each had his own chime. One holiday we heard the bells of Mr. Wasylyshen, the neighbor from across the river. He was in a hurry and his team was coming at full gallop, the bells chiming gloriously.

"Whatever could be the matter!" Mama exclaimed. She sent one of us to get Papa, and ran to meet Mr. Wasylyshen who had jumped from his sleigh and was running toward the house.

I heard Mama say, "I'll come right over. Is it safe to cross the river?" (It was half a mile to cross the river and four miles by the road.)

"Oh, yes," he answered. "I came that way."

Running to his waiting team, Mr. Wasylyshen grabbed the reins and off he went with bells ringing and snow flying from the pounding hoofs of running horses.

Papa came up from the blacksmith shop. Mama said to him, "I have to go to Mrs. Wasylyshen. Go hitch the team, quick!"

By the time Mama had changed her dress and put on her coat, Papa had the cutter at the door and they were on their way. Our team was not as fast as Mr. Wasylyshen's team. He had the fastest team in the neighborhood and the prettiest chiming bells.

As usual when Mama and Papa were gone, we children took up the challenge to surprise them upon their return. Excitedly, we began with our plans. We wanted to surprise Mama by having all the work done when she got home. The woodbox and water barrel would be filled, the bare board floors scrubbed and anything else we could think to do. It was so much fun to surprise Mama and Papa because they showed such pleasure and appreciation. However, this time, not much had been done before we heard the jingling bells of the horses.

Mama rushed into the house and began to pull off her coat. "Mrs. Wasylyshen had twin babies," she said. "She didn't expect them so soon and she didn't expect twins. She has no clothes for them, and nothing to make any with. I'll have to make some kind of layette. The babies are so tiny and may not live. The little girl is doing better than the boy is. I left those babies wrapped in some of their dad's clean underwear."

I followed Mama upstairs and watched her pull the flannel sheets from my bed. She began to sew gowns, diapers, bands, and undershirts - a complete layette for each tiny baby. When all was ready, she and Papa went back across the river. We children did the milking and other chores plus a few extra things before Mama and Papa returned much later that night. The little boy had died.   I cannot remember if Mama took flannel sheets from any of the other beds, but Alma and I had to sleep with summer cotton sheets for the rest of the winter. Our house had no insulation and was heated with a "central heater" fed with chunks of wood. At night, a thin layer of ice formed in the wash basin. On windy nights, snow drifted through the cracks around the windows onto the bed covers, but did us no harm. We had Mama's homemade wool quilts that kept us snug and warm.

Chapter 4

More Providential Experiences
Childhood to Marriage

Where Were the Cows?

The Lord is thy keeper: the Lord is thy shade upon thy right hand. The Lord shall preserve thee from all evil.

Psalm 121:5-7

Soon after my conversion, I had my first experience in answered prayer that really impressed me. After my third excursion to the pasture in search of the cows, I grew weary and said to Mama, "I just can't find those cows! I have hunted everywhere and I can't hear any bell. Petsy must be lying down."

Petsy was the bell cow and carried her job with dignity. She insisted her place was at the head of the line on the path. She claimed first place at the smoky smudge fire we made to keep mosquitoes away while we milked. Now Petsy had let me down. And it was getting dark. At night we could hear the coyotes howling and I was afraid Mama would send me out again.

"You know it is not good for the cows not to be milked, Myrtle," Mama said to me. "I know you are tired. Maybe the cows got out of the pasture. Get on old Rock and go down the east road to look for them."

With the growing darkness and many misgivings, I jumped on old Rock, our horse, and went in search once more. While riding down the road, it occurred to me that Jesus might care about me and my problem. I prayed, "Dear Heavenly Father, Thou knowest where the cows are. I will let go of the reins and please lead Rock to them. In Jesus' name I pray. Amen."

Now, you know, when a horse has his freedom from the reins, especially old Rock, he starts for home. Rock did not head for home or even hint at it. He seemed in a hurry to go further down the road. Then to my horror, he headed toward a ditch and a path surrounded by bushes and darkness. I thought, "I must let him go." But my fears overcame my faith when he entered the blackness. I grabbed the reins and headed for home.

The next morning, about an hour after sunrise, Mama sent me out once again on old Rock. I headed down the east road, carefully avoiding the dark corner so I would not have to acknowledge my cowardice should I find the cows there. When I came to the gate at the far end of the pasture, I thought to pray again. I asked the Lord to forgive me for my fear and to please guide Rock to the cows.

I let go of the reins. Rock, never known to hurry, tore through the bushes at near gallop. I hung onto his mane determined not to touch the reins again. Branches scratched my legs. Tall grass cut through the skin, but I hung on and watched in dismay as Rock headed for the corner near the ditch of the night before. Even before I saw them I could hear Petsy's bell. Old Joe, the dog who had raced beside us enjoying the competition with Rock, began to round up every cow. Soon we were on the path to home with Petsy in the lead.

Strangely, Rock was no longer in a hurry. I had to urge him along to keep up. Soon the cows were relieved of their milk load and I had learned a precious lesson on trusting the Lord.

God Knows How to Do
Math and Composition

In the day of my trouble I will call upon thee: for thou wilt answer me.

Psalm 86:7

During my school years, even in high school, I struggled with algebra. It seemed there were some problems that I could not solve regardless of how much I studied. I loved school and worked hard to do well. Up through the eighth grade I attended a one-room school. There was always homework in nearly every subject. After walking the two miles from school and doing my afternoon chores, I had about two hours for study. Since algebra was my most difficult subject, I did it last. Sometimes I went to bed without the answer. Then I would pray. Oftentimes I dreamed how to work out the problem and would remember it the next morning.

Once in high school we were having an important final exam on composition. I had studied hard and did quite well until I came to the last item asking for a composition, including an outline, on any one from a number of topics. I seemed to get no thoughts about any of them. Even the most promising topic, "On Writing Examinations" seemed hopeless to me. With time running out, I began to pray. Then a thought came - divide it up and write about those who study for an exam and those who do not, and the results for each. Words began flowing. We had been taught to do the outline first, but the thoughts were coming so fast that I just wrote. Afterwards I went over it and made my outline.

The teacher said it was the best composition she had ever received. She read it to the entire class and detailed all the features that made it good. I had not thought of any of them. I just wrote what Jesus put on my mind.

School Clothes

And why take ye thought for raiment? Consider the lilies of the field, how they grow; they toil not, neither do they spin: And yet I say unto you, that even Solomon in all his glory was not arrayed like one of these.

Matthew 6:28-29

My sister, Pearl, a registered nurse, came home for Christmas one year while I was still in grade school. She told me so many interesting things about her work that I, too, decided to become a nurse. Those were the depression years and times were hard. After the eighth grade I went to work as a hired girl in homes. I would work a year then go to school for a year. Grades nine and ten were taken by correspondence with books being the only cost. I stayed home to study. For the eleventh grade, I worked for a family in Dauphin for my room and board. The previous summer, I earned enough money for books and some fabric. Mama used the fabric to make me a skirt and blouse. These served as my only school clothes until graduation. I washed them out by hand over the weekend. Since the blouse was thin enough to dry overnight, I was able to wash it during the week.

I grew tired of wearing that same outfit but there was no other way. One day toward the end of the school year, my married sister, Lois came for a visit and met me on the steps at school. She said, "Myrtle, you look so lovely in that skirt and blouse. It really does something for you."

That was what I needed to finish the year. I was taking grade eleven matriculation, equal to grade twelve in the United States. The year was 1938 and time for my graduation. Someone gave my mother a used dress that my sister, Annie, a dressmaker altered to fit me. Since graduation was not a great event in that high school, the dress was all I needed.

Though it was a great financial struggle all the way through high school, I learned much that helped prepare me for the future. It is amazing what "necessities" one can do without when there is no money available for them.

Healed of Quinsy

Heal me, O Lord, and I shall be healed; save me, and I shall be saved; for thou art my praise

Jeremiah 17:14

During my last year in high school, I became very ill with quinsy. This is an abscess on one or both tonsils. Mine was on both. For three days I fretted about having to miss school, but then I became so ill that nothing mattered. My throat was extremely sore. Breathing grew difficult, and I could hardly eat or drink. As I lay in bed, everything around me seemed to fade away. Through a feverish haze, I heard, "I've just called your mother and she said to call Dr. Rogers right away. You are a very sick girl."

That was Ella Harkness speaking. She was a trained nurse and I was working in her home for my room and board. When Dr. Rogers, our family physician arrived, my fever was up to 104 degrees. I barely remember his visit then or any of the later visits. He wanted to hospitalize me, but since we could not afford it, Ella, an excellent nurse, said she would care for me in her home.

About all I remember for the next few days was Ella coming in to change the foment on my throat. I did hear the doctor say I had quinsy. I knew a neighbor who had died with quinsy, but even this thought did not rouse me from my lethargy.

Three or four days later, I heard Dr. Rogers say that my tonsils were almost ready to be lanced. Early the next morning I felt something pop in my throat. The abscess had broken. The pain was relieved and my breathing became easier. Without antibodies or sulfa drugs, which were not yet available, I had experienced a healing miracle. The Lord did the healing, but He used Ella in the process. Every hour, night and day, she had changed the foment. With her alarm clock beside her, she napped in her rocking chair near the kitchen stove while keeping a basin of water boiling. Each hour when the alarm went off, she squeezed out the woolen cloth and brought it steaming hot to put on my throat. She then covered the hot cloth with a piece of toweling, then oilcloth.

After I graduated from nursing school, I worked in the Dauphin General Hospital for two years. Foments were a standard treatment for boils, abscesses and infected sores. Remembering what Ella and the Lord had done for me, never did I miss an hour in changing the foments, even when there were several patients using them.

Chapter 5

Still More Providential Experiences Childhood to Marriage

Getting into Nurses Training

Trust in the Lord with all thine heart; and lean not unto thine own understanding. In all thy ways acknowledge him, and he shall direct thy paths.

Proverbs 3:5-6

The summer after my high school graduation, my sister, Pearl came home for a visit. I had been accepted for nurses training at the William Mason Memorial Hospital in Kentucky where she had done her training and was now a supervisor. Plans were for me to go back with her. However, the hospital had burned down in 1935 and had to be rebuilt. It had not been replaced on the government's approved list, and I was unable to get a student visa to enter the United States. Because of this, my training was delayed for a year. This turned out to be a blessing. The groundwork I did in getting the hospital approved enabled other girls from Canada to get visas for training there. A girl from Saskatchewan, Viola Neufeld, who had been accepted in 1939 as I had, corresponded with me while we waited. When we got into training at the hospital, she became my roommate. The next year her sister joined us. Upon our return to Canada, I met their brother and in 1946 we were married.

While I waited for government approval and my visa, I stayed in Winnipeg, the capital city where the United States consul's office was located. For several months I worked as a housekeeper. When the lady decided to stop work and keep her own home, I had to look for another job. I answered several ads and was told I lacked the housekeeping experience that was needed for serving at big parties.

I did not know what to do. My job would end in a few days. The big city frightened me. It looked like I might have to return to Dauphin when I spotted a newspaper ad with the heading, "Are you a girl in trouble? We can help you."

Surely this was meant for me. I had no job and needed to stay near the consul to get my visa (this had to be done in person). Making my way to the address in the paper, I walked up to an ordinary looking, ill-kept house and yard. Gathering courage, I went inside where I found several young girls sitting on various steps of the stairway. Gingerly, I took the bottom step.

I began to feel uneasy. As I listened to their conversations, I grew more insecure. One or two left for a room upstairs. My uneasiness continued to grow. Surely an angel was at my side impressing me that this was not the place for me and my kind of trouble.

Quickly rising, I went outside and back to the house where I worked. That night in my room, I had a special prayer time. I told the Lord my situation and how frightened I was. I asked Him to guide me. Then I opened my Bible and my eyes fell on Proverbs 3:5-6. From memory, I recalled something the king of Great Britain gave in a New Year's speech when I was a teenager. "I said to the man who stood at the gate of the year, 'Give me a light that I may walk safely into the unknown.' And he said to me, 'Put your hand into the hand of God. That will be to you better than light and safer than the known way."

The Lord did not say to me, "Stay in Winnipeg" or, "Go back to Dauphin" but to acknowledge Him. My mind was immediately at peace. I went to sleep and the next morning there was no question as to what I should do. I was to return home.

I found work in Dauphin but the pay was very low. When my visa finally came through, there was no money for bus fare to Kentucky. Pearl paid thirty-one dollars for my tuition, which included books and uniforms. But, from her meager salary, she could not help with the bus fare. There was only one way. Petsy, the bell cow and best milker, had to be sold. With extreme gratitude to my parents for their sacrifice, I left for Murray, Kentucky to begin training at the William Mason Memorial Hospital on May 31, 1939 under the supervision of my sister. I left home with one best dress and one everyday dress. The first thing Pearl did was to take me to a store and buy me two lovely dresses. I really don't know how I would have managed without them over the next three years.

Nursing school was very pleasant and went quickly for me. Pearl, nine years my senior, was a special blessing. She was a mother-sister to me in my homesick days. While in training, the William Mason Memorial Hospital paid each student five dollars per month, plus room and board. However, when we had to spend nine months affiliating at the Louisville General Hospital, it was without pay. Money was scarce, but again, the Lord provided and I was able to graduate in 1942.

My passing of the state boards was definitely an answer to prayer. During the exams I panicked and literally prayed my way through the four days of grueling tests. I finished at the top in a class of twelve. My friend, Viola Neufeld came in a close second.

Courtship and Marriage

But who am I, and what is my people, that we should be able to offer so willingly after this sort? For all things come of thee, and of thine own have we given thee.

I Chronicles 29:14

Everything in life is providential. The farmer sows the seed, but without God, the seed will not germinate. Martin Luther says that while the man sleeps, the seed is growing. We work and earn money, but that is not what feeds us. Does not God provide the strength for our work and make the seed to grow? Do not *all things come of thee, and of thine own have we given thee?"* (I Chronicles 29:14)

After graduation from nurses training, I went back to Dauphin for two years. My roommate, Viola, went to work at the Rest Haven Sanitarium (not TB) and Hospital on Vancouver Island. A year later her sister, Elizabeth, graduated and joined her. After two years in Dauphin, I joined them. That is how I became acquainted with their family and brother, Ray. After several visits to the Island with the family, it became apparent that Ray's visits were more for seeing me than to see his sisters. We began courting, and in 1946 we were married. I would like to share how God answered prayer and provided for my wedding.

In those days, the pay for nurses was not much. With what little I made, I was helping my younger sister through school and trying to save for some post-graduate work. This left me with no money for a wedding. Like all girls, I wanted a wedding. My parents were able to give me twenty-five dollars. That money alone, I thought, could not stretch far enough. For two years I had been paying income tax, but had not received any returns. I pleaded with the Lord to cause that money to come. He did provide, but not according to my timetable. He had His plans all arranged and the twenty-five dollars was all we spent for our wedding.

In John 2 we read about the marriage at Cana and how Jesus turned the water into wine for the wedding feast. This tells me that Jesus is interested in the happiness of young people and their wedding. For our wedding, I am certain that He was. We were surrounded with beautiful flowers and loving people.

Because of circumstances in getting our visas, we were married across the US/Canada border in Bellingham, Washington. In preparation for the ceremony, we went to see a minister at the Seventh-day Adventist Church in Bellingham. He was very kind and helpful. He suggested that we have a small wedding at the church. Stan's wife, Merle, loaned me her wedding dress for my "something borrowed." Viola served as bride's maid and my only attendant. She was able to use her formal from a required event at the time of our graduation from nursing school. It was a lovely dress and served well for my wedding. Ray's brother, Henry, was the best man. Stan gave me away since my parents could not come. We did not have a Bible boy or flower girl and left out the reception.   Since we knew no one in Bellingham, the minister announced our wedding plans at their Sabbath services and members came to our wedding on Sunday. The back half of the church was closed off to create a cozy atmosphere. The minister's wife sang a couple of solos, and a lady from the church decorated with fresh flowers from her garden.   Her ministry was to decorate the church each week for the Sabbath, which she had done, but she chose to redecorate for our wedding.

Not only did the church members come, they gave us gifts of money and easy to pack items. They also gave us a book with their names. What a beautiful memory to hang in our memory hall!   We also had several family members present.

Chapter 6

Providential Experiences
Marriage and Beyond

College and Medical School

But my God shall supply all your need according to his riches in glory by Christ Jesus.

Philippians 4:19

Ray's desire was to be a medical doctor. After our wedding, we went to the college where he was in his third year of pre-med school. I took some classes toward my Bachelor of Science degree in nursing while he continued working toward his degree. Toward the end of the year, we met some missionaries on furlough from Africa. With our growing acquaintance, they decided Ray and I should go back to Africa with them to help in the mission. We were just the couple they wanted. We gave it careful thought and presented it to the Lord in prayer. Even though medical school was important to Ray, we were willing to go to Africa if this was the Lord's will for us. We talked it over and decided to

43

leave it in the Lord's hands to close the door to medical school.

World War II had just ended and many were applying for admission to the College of Medical Evangelists (now Loma Linda University). Competition was keen. If we were not accepted, we would go to Africa. We were accepted.

The next hurdle was a down payment for medical school. We had both been working all year, but made only enough for our tuition and living expenses. My visa needed to be changed from student to permanent so I could work full time. This called for a return trip to Canada. We decided to go forward with that, and if no down payment came, we would consider the door to medical school closed.

Two days before we left for California, a cousin came to visit. Appalled at the possibility that the lack of funds would keep Ray from medical school, he said, "I have a small savings, a little more than you need. I'll loan you the down payment."

This was our open door to medical school. There was a great demand for registered nurses and the hospital connected with the medical school had already written me asking me to work there. I was put in charge of the 30-crib newborn nursery. Ray worked in an emergency lab three nights each week. He slept at the lab and was on call. Many times he was able to sleep all night. He also had some time to study. This was a great arrangement for him. Within the first year, we were able to repay the loan, even though we had to count and plan every penny we spent. We learned much about money management.   Every two weeks when we were paid, we sat down together and planned for our financial needs.   We began with the Lord's tithe, one tenth of our income.   Next, we paid the tuition for the two weeks, then my uniforms, etc.   We allowed eleven dollars for food.   The day after payday, we went grocery shopping.   Ray totaled the bill as we selected the items.   When we reached eleven dollars, we stopped.   I remember one time we ate oats with gravy for four days.   But, we ended medical school with very little debt.

Starting a Family

Who knoweth not in all these that the hand of the Lord hath wrought this? In whose hand is the soul of every living thing, and the breath of all mankind.

Job 12:9-10

At the beginning of the second year in medical school, we started thinking about a family. I was over thirty and getting on toward the old side for having children. As a worker at the hospital, I had insurance coverage. Also, obstetricians did not charge medical students for delivery of babies. But how would we manage without me working when the baby came? We sat down and figured it out.

Each year, I was allowed two weeks vacation that could be carried over. With two years, I would have four weeks of paid vacation. For the last two weeks of the six weeks needed for maternity leave, we decided to go by faith.

My work at the hospital nursery was busy but light. This allowed me to work until three days before the baby was born. About that time, I received the long overdue income tax return payment from Canada for which I had so earnestly prayed before our wedding. It was enough, plus a little extra, for the last two weeks of leave. Once again, our heavenly Father had provided at exactly the right time.

When our daughter Betty Rae was born, she did not breathe or cry. Anxiously I waited and prayed, but I felt at peace. She had to be put on a respiratory machine with oxygen. Student nurses had sneaked in from their wards as soon as they heard I had been admitted. I had taught most of them nursery technique and we loved each other. They crowded into my room to wish me well before hurrying back to their various duties. When word got out about the baby, a student nurse looked in and said to me, "All the students on duty are going to meet right now and have special prayer for her." Very soon Betty Rae began to breathe on her own.

Three months before graduation, we welcomed our son Robert. After graduation, we returned to Canada for the intern year. When Ray finished with his internship, he was invited to practice in his hometown of Waldheim, Saskatchewan. Our Patty was born there.

After five years in Waldheim, we moved to Vancouver Island for five years. Ray was medical director of the Rest Haven Sanitarium and Hospital where I had worked when we met. Our second son Henry joined our family during our first year on the Island.

Saved by Angels

For he shall give his angels charge over thee, to keep thee in all thy ways.

Psalm 91:11

When Henry was about a year old, we went down to Loma Linda for the post-graduate convention. At that time, the speed limits were seventy miles per hour and car doors opened opposite to what they do now. Also, we did not have seat belts. I was in the front seat with Henry sitting in my lap. Suddenly we went around a curve and my coat sleeve caught the door handle. The door flew open and we swerved toward the opening. I thought Henry and I were both going to fly out and hit the pavement. Then it seemed that we were being pushed back inside the car. It was not a touch that could be felt, but a gentle force. And then the door closed. I am grateful our angels were doing faithful guard duty that day.

God Cares for Boys and Their Pets

He shall call upon me, and I will answer him.

Psalm 91:15

After spending the five years in Rest Haven and two in the United States, we went to the Chiapas Mountains in southern Mexico where we joined a self-supporting mission group that worked mainly with the Chamula Indians. For the trip to Mexico, we packed all the household goods we could into a trailer, including a washing machine. Our son Robert had a little fox terrier named Specky that he dearly loved. We were told if we had an updated shot certificate from a veterinarian, we would likely be able to take the dog into Mexico. After driving fifty miles out of our way in an unsuccessful search for a vet, we warned Robert that we might have to leave Specky at the border. We had prayed about it and knew we must be honest in all our dealings with the custom officials. When we were ready to cross the border, we instructed Robert to let the dog sit on his lap in plain view. We told him that Jesus was interested in both him and his pet, and if it were His will, Specky would get across. It would be the same with all our things.

At the border, we were asked about the contents of the trailer and explained that it was our household goods. After debating, the official decided against having us unload the trailer. When he looked into the back seat of the station wagon, he patted Specky on the head and instructed us to continue our journey.

Once again the Lord had provided and He made a young boy very happy.

Chapter 7

Providential Experiences In Mexico

Henry and the Measles

Even a child is known by his doings, whether his work be pure, and whether it be right.

Proverbs 20:11

While we were in the Chiapas mountains, a measles epidemic broke out in the nearby village of Rincon. Many were dying. They sent to our clinic for help. Although nurses and helpers were in short supply, we sent as many as we could to give penicillin and help with treatments. Our older children, Betty Rae and Robert had returned to the states for school. Patty, who was twelve at the time, went to Rincon every day to help. She wanted to be a nurse and this was a great experience for her. The need was so great, the nurses taught her to give shots and helped her to learn how to do treatments. At the time, Henry was only eight but he begged for permission to go help. I knew he could be useful in helping to carry food, water and run errands, but he had never had the measles.

He kept saying, "Mama, please let me go. Patty is helping and I want to help, too."

"But, Henry, Patty has had the measles. You haven't. I don't want my little boy to die." I told him.

His answer stunned me, "Jesus gave His life for me, and why shouldn't I give my life for the Chamulas?"

I had no answer to that. The next day, Henry went with the group. He was a great help. He also got the measles which made him extremely ill. We thought he truly was going to give his life for the Chamulas. We provided nursing care, treatments and penicillin, but Jesus did the healing. Henry made it and the glory goes to God.

A Mexican Angel?

Are they not all ministering spirits, sent forth to minister for them who shall be heirs of salvation?

Hebrews 1:14

Our trips through Mexico were always an adventure. We never knew what would happen. All we could do was commit to the Lord and trust His promise in Psalm 121:8, *"The Lord shall preserve thy going out and thy coming in from this time forth, and even for evermore."*

On our first trip through, we went into a large city looking for gas. We knew very little Spanish at that time. Most of our needs and wants had to be made known through body language, such as hand motions, etc. Through motions and by standing beside the tank, we were able to get our gas, but when we asked for directions back to the highway from which we came, we got nowhere. It was getting late and we were anxious to make the next small town before dark. Just as we were about to give up, a car drove in.

In English, the driver said, "May I help you?"

We explained our situation and he said, "Just follow me."

With that, he led us here and there until we began to wonder about him. Then he stopped and directed us on how to get to the next junction. We called out our thanks as he jumped into his car, turned around and sped away. We had gone far out of our way and felt the Lord sent that man to us to get back on track. But was he a Mexican who had learned English, or was he an angel in Mexican guise?

A Luxury Hotel - Free

For so he giveth his beloved sleep.

Psalm 127:2

We had our immigration visas but had not applied for citizenship in the United States. In order to keep our visas, we had to return to the US once a year. Also, to stay in Mexico, every six months we had to go to a border for our re-entry permit. The nearest borderpoint for the re-entry permit was Guatemala. Upon the return trip to our mission station, Yerba Buena, evening would come. Unable to afford motels, we usually slept in our car. We had been advised to pull into all-night gas stations and ask if we could park and sleep there. The attendants were always willing, but on this particular night, we had misjudged the distance. We were on a road with little traffic. We knew it wasn't safe to stay beside the road. Ray stopped to consider what we should do. A car pulled up. This frightened us. We soon discovered that the driver was an American. He asked if he could help. When we said we had no place to spend the night, he said, "Come to my place. I have a ranch, but it is about fifty miles off the road."

So, once again, we found ourselves following a stranger. This seemed the thing for us to do. Had we not been praying for a safe place?

The man led us into beautiful country with tall trees. In the pitch blackness of night, on and on we went. Finally, he drove into the entrance of his luxurious home. He took us to a separate bungalow reserved for guests. The next morning, after a restful sleep, we were awakened by the exotic singing of birds. It was like a taste of heaven. Everything we could wish for had been provided and our host would not take a cent for the accommodations.

We Don't Watch Over Ourselves

The angel of the Lord encampeth round about them that fear him, and delivereth them.

Psalm 34:7

There was another time when we found night upon us with no service station in sight. Ray became so sleepy he could not continue to drive. This time no one came along to help us. The Lord had another lesson of trust to teach us.

Ray climbed into the back of the station wagon to stretch out. I could drive, but had no license. We decided that I should sit in the driver's seat, and if I heard anyone coming, start driving. Service stations were well lighted all night and I could knit to stay awake, but here, sitting still in the darkness, I became very sleepy. Out on this dark, lonely road, I found myself dozing and soon realized I could not stay awake. I had always been petrified when it was dark. I asked the Lord to keep me awake and then the thought struck me. "Am I trusting God to care for us? Or am I trusting in my weak, helpless, sleepy self to care for us? Can not God take care of us with me asleep as well as with me awake?"

My extreme fear left. Peacefully, I slept while sitting behind the wheel until Ray woke up to drive us on. I told my family about my prayer and experience. I have never since suffered from such fear. We are so often inclined to trust partly in God and partly in ourselves. I must add that I do not believe we should be presumptuous. Jesus would not jump off the temple. We should take the precautions He expects, but He is the One who keeps us.

Chapter 8

The Guyana Story - I

The Call

Also I heard the voice of the Lord, saying, Whom shall I send, and who will go for us? Then said I, Here am I; send me."

Isaiah 6:8

We had left Mexico and were living in Wildwood, Georgia when we received a call from the secretary of the General Conference of the Seventh-day Adventist Church to go to Guyana in South America. It was an emergency call. The chief medical officer went on leave, and his assistant came up with an old law that said only doctors with a British license could practice in Guyana. He sent notice for the attending physician, *Dr. Potter to leave at once. However, permission was granted for Dr. Potter to stay until another physician could be found.

Since Ray still had his medical license in British Columbia, we were asked to go. Ray would be the medical director for a fifty-bed hospital in Georgetown, the capital. For many years we had longed for mission service overseas and were excited about this call.

What a rush! We had only one month to make preparations. We had visas to get, packing and shipping to do, all while Ray continued carrying out his present medical duties. Finally, we were on our way, flying over the Caribbean Sea and countries of breathtaking beauty. The coral islands were especially pretty. On August 9, 1971 we arrived in Guyana. Only one thing marred our happiness. On the trip, Ray began having bowel obstruction problems. He was born with an extra loop of bowel, and periodically, this loop would twist. We had always been able to get it to untwist. The excitement, our hasty departure, and the sugared drinks served on the plane had their effect. The loop would not untwist.

The Surgery

O Lord our Lord, how excellent is thy name in all the earth! who hast set thy glory above the heavens. When I consider thy heavens, the work of thy fingers, the moon and the stars, which thou has ordained; what is man, that thou art mindful of him? and the son of man, that thou visitest him?

Psalm 8:3-4

In spite of intense pain, Ray worked for one day after our arrival in Guyana. All that night, I was up with him trying our usual remedies. Nothing worked. At 5:00 A.M., I called Dr. Potter who was scheduled to leave that morning. When I explained the situation, he decided to stay for another day, yet he failed to recognize the severity of Ray's condition. He thought Ray was suffering from culture shock, which often comes to new missionaries. He gave him pain medicine, a sedative and said all he needed was rest.

There is a saying in the medical profession, "never let the sun rise or set on a bowel obstruction." This sedative put Ray in a deep but troubled sleep for the day. When he woke that evening with unbearable pain, I again called Dr. Potter. Still thinking culture shock, he gave Ray some castor oil and hot vegetable soup which he fixed and administered himself. Later, Dr. Potter confessed and apologized for his error in judgement and said had he known we served four years in Mexico he would have reacted differently. Shortly after taking the castor oil and soup, Ray appeared to be in shock. I called Dr. Potter and insisted something be done. He and his colleague, *Dr. Marino (also leaving Guyana) took Ray to the hospital for x-rays. It was now around 10:00 P.M. As soon as possible, I followed and met Dr. Potter coming from X-ray. He said, "This is very serious. We will have to operate immediately."

My heart rose into my throat and I said, "I must go tell Henry."

Sternly, Dr. Potter snapped, "Don't you dare wake up that boy!"

I knew that was best, but Henry was fourteen years old and the only other person I knew in this strange land. In a panic, I ran outside. There before me was the most glorious sight. The heavens were aflame with stars. There is not a more beautiful sight in all the world than the stars in the southern sky! In my heart, I cried out, "O Lord, Thou art there!" The sight of the stars, with their message, gave me what human help could not. My panic faded. The God who holds up the stars could surely hold me up. (Later, I learned that the Southern Cross always shone right above our house.)

I went back into the hospital and calmly walked upstairs where Ray was being taken into surgery. As a registered nurse, I was granted permission to go in and observe. This gave assurance to Ray, and was providential, for I observed first hand the surgical accident that since has given so much trouble.

The surgery was progressing nicely until undue pressure from the castor oil caused an instrument to slip, and the abdominal cavity filled with contamination. Dr. Potter and his staff worked diligently to clean the cavity and proceeded with the suturing. Dr. Potter was about to close up the incision when he was called away by a midwife to deal with an obstetrical emergency. One by one the members of the assisting team were called away also. I was left with the scrub nurse in her sterile gown and gloves, and Ray sleeping on the surgery table with no anesthetic to keep him that way. The incision was wide open. I felt panic rising. The scrub nurse sensed this.

She quietly picked up a sterile towel, put some saline tablets in a basin and said, "Mrs. Neufeld, would you please get me some hot sterile water from the tank?"

Immediately, the nurse in me responded. I became the nurse rather than the wife of the patient. My panic left. I knew exactly what to do and began doing it. The scrub nurse wrung out a sterile towel and laid it over the incision. I noted the anaesthetic bag and squeezed it periodically as I had seen the anesthetist do, hoping to keep Ray asleep. Half an hour elapsed before the doctors returned to finished the surgery without further mishap.

It is hard to express my feelings. That night, my husband lived, but the mother and her baby died. This was her twelfth baby.

After the Operation

Fear thou not; for I am with thee: be not dismayed; for I am thy God: I will strengthen thee; yea, I will help thee; yea, I will uphold thee with the right hand of my righteousness.

Isaiah 41:10

The next morning, when Henry awoke and found no one home, he came to the hospital looking for us. No one wanted to tell him of his dad's condition. When directed to the nurse's office, he was told to go to Room 109. When he walked in, I looked up and said, "Daddy had surgery last night. He is very sick."

Henry took the news calmly, just as I thought he would. For the next two weeks, he spent most of his time alone while his dad hung on to life by a thread. There were times when Ray asked to be let go, saying, "I can't take it any longer." The Lord always gave me an encouraging word for him. For this reason, I felt I could not leave Ray's bedside to be with Henry, and Henry understood this. I was grateful to the maintenance workers, the gardeners, the guards, and Mr. Wright with his donkey, Tarzan. They became Henry's friends and helped to pass the time while we waited for Ray to get well and our household goods to arrive with Henry's books. The goods were six months in coming. Fortunately, Henry had his trumpet for practice, which helped.

Everyone was very kind to us during those weeks. Dr. Potter stayed and worked hard to save Ray's life. The nursing staff worked faithfully. The assistant to the chaplain spent much time with me. Often she would just sit in silent sympathy. A very special and loving relationship developed between us and the people that lasted over the next seven years. It was a happy day when on August 25, 1971 Dr. Potter said Ray could have some clear broth. "Well," I said, "I think you should serve it in a silver cup since this is our silver wedding anniversary."

Dr. Potter spread the news. At shift change, the nurses brought a decorated wedding cake and fruit juice to our room. Though Ray could not eat it, this was special for us. Another treasured memory to hang in our memory hall. We did not have a cake at our wedding since we had no reception.

Chapter 9

The Guyana Story - II

The Letter

And it shall come to pass, that before they call, I will answer; and while they are yet speaking, I will hear.

Isaiah 65:24

Before Ray recovered, I was concerned that our children in the states knew nothing of their father's condition. Aware that I could phone, I thought the cost prohibitive. A few days before Dr. Potter left, I sat by Ray's bed thinking there was no hope and wondering what to do. I decided to write a letter and explain the situation to Ray's brother, Don, an ordained minister. He lived near Washington, DC. I asked him to notify the children. When the crisis was over, Dr. Potter made preparation to return to the states. I asked that upon his arrival in Miami, would he please call Don with the good news.

When Don received my letter, he notified the children, then took the letter upstairs to his bedroom, knelt down, and spread the letter out before the Lord.   (2 Kings 19:14-16 *"And Hezekiah received the letter of the hand of the messengers, and read it; and Hezekiah went up into the house of the Lord, and spread it before the Lord.   And Hezekiah prayed before the Lord."*

Don had not begun to pray when the phone rang. Dr. Potter was calling from Miami to tell him the crisis with Ray was over. Now Don could bring the good news to our children.

The Follow-Up

*Who knoweth not in all these that the hand of the
LORD hath wrought this?*

Job 12:9

With Doctors Potter and Marino gone and Ray still
a patient, what was the hospital to do?   It was
decided that there would be no outpatient care and
Ray would give orders from his room until a relief
doctor could be found.   However, we encountered a
problem. Not only was a British license required, but
also we discovered Ray's British Columbia license
was unacceptable.   It had to be from certain
provinces in Canada.   Saskatchewan was one of
those, but while in British Columbia, Ray had allowed
his Saskatchewan license to expire. This would have
been one of the few acceptable provinces from
Canada.   The hospital manager called me to his
office and asked if I knew of anyone who could
intercede with the registrar in Saskatchewan and get
the license reactivated. Yes, I did. The president of
the Manitoba-Saskatchewan. Conference was a very
good friend. *Pastor Simpson was more than happy
to help.   Surprisingly soon, a telegram arrived to
verify Ray was licensed in Saskatchewan and the
license would be forthcoming via airmail with a letter
to follow.

In the letter, we saw the hand of God who knows the end from the beginning. Years before, He had prepared for this emergency. First, by having us intern and become licensed in Saskatchewan and in having Pastor Simpson in the president's office. Next, imagine our surprise to find that the registrar was *Dr. Dunsmore, the surgeon under whom Ray did his internship! Dr. Dunsmore had also assisted in all the surgeries we did while at Waldheim. We knew him well and were very good friends. The letter also stated that Pastor Simpson had paid the renewal fee of $250.00 to prevent further delay. We could now reimburse this fee. Meanwhile, Ray could give orders for the patients in the hospital.

A few days later, the hospital manager met me in the hall and said, "We just got word that a *Dr. Robman has consented to come for a month. He has the right Canadian license."

I nearly jumped for joy. "I know him." I said. "He was the doctor at Rest Haven. I worked with him for nearly two years."

Dr. Robman had not been there long when Ray obstructed again and had to be hospitalized. This was from the infection caused by the surgical accident. Ray was soon allowed to go home even though he was not doing well. I wrote to share the whole news with my brothers and sisters. I ended my letter by saying, "I don't see how he can live like this. I feel so alone here."

You Are Not Alone

I will not fail thee, nor forsake thee.

Joshua 1:5

About a week after I sent the letter, the phone rang. I could not believe it when I heard a familiar voice say, "This is your brother, Stan. I just called to let you know you are not alone. We are all with you."

We talked of other things but these were the words that I remember. Later that same day, the doorbell rang and there stood someone from the florist with a lovely tropical flower arrangement. The note said, 'from your sister, Lois, to let you know you are not alone.'

My cup runneth over in gratitude to my loving heavenly Father. I sometimes forget He is an ever-present God.

Anointed

Is any sick among you? let him call for the elders of the church; and let them pray over him, anointing him with oil in the name of the Lord: And the prayer of faith shall save the sick, and the Lord shall raise him up; and if he has committed sins, they shall be forgiven him.

James 5:14-15

When the month was up and Dr. Robman had to return to the United States, another doctor, *Dr. Forest arrived for a six-week term. Ray was getting weaker. He ate and slept little. One day he asked for anointing and prayer according to the instruction in James. This was a very solemn service. Although there was not an instant healing, Ray slept soundly that night and was able to eat the next day. Soon he went to his office and could work with the assistance of Dr. Forest.   At the end of his six-week term, Dr. Forest left Ray to work alone. He was on call seven days a week, day and night.

Over the next seven years, we were privileged to have help from USA doctors for short periods of time.   The Chief Medical officer of Guyana had returned from his leave of absence and again shelved the old law that had prevented US licensed doctors from working in our hospital.   However, there were none to be found that could stay permanently, but we were pleased to have the short term help. Twice, we had help for more than a year. Only God and us know how many times in those seven years Ray slipped home during office hours to take a warm bath to help release an obstruction before returning to his office. A year after his first surgery, he had to be flown to the states for another operation. This time, they found that he had the beginnings of Crohn's disease. Still, we served in Guyana for another six years.

Chapter 10

The Guyana Story - III

Mr. Ali

Be still, and know that I am God; I will be exalted among the heathen, I will be exalted in the earth.

Psalm 46:10

One day while walking down the second floor hall of the hospital, I was startled by loud voices. A man was arguing angrily. Interspersed were the pleading voices of ladies.

I asked one of the nurses, "Who is it? What is the trouble?"

As I approached, I could see a man in a wheel chair looking very perturbed. She said, "His name is Mr. Ali. He is dying of cancer and is to be admitted for care but he wants a private room. We don't have any. We will have one this afternoon but he refuses to go into a semi-private until then. He wants them to take him home."

And home he went, but was soon back. This time willing to go into any room because his pain was so great. He was given something for his pain and later put in a private room. This happened in the middle of the week. Sabbath came and, as usual, when the sun went down, Ray went over to make rounds, visiting the more seriously ill patients. I usually went with him but this Saturday night, I had too many things to do.

"I won't go tonight," I told him.

He went alone. After he was gone for a while, I felt impressed to go anyway. Quickly, I ran over and met Ray ready to come home.

"How is Mr. Ali?" I asked.

"I don't know," he answered. "I thought I wouldn't see him this time."

"I want to see him." I said. "Let's go, and maybe he will let us sing for him."

Ray asked, "What could we sing, seeing as he is a Hindu and doesn't believe in Jesus?"

"We could sing, 'Be still and Know That I Am God." I responded.

We entered the room. Mr. Ali was pleased to see us. His family was also there. After asking him how he felt, Ray asked, "Would you like us to sing for you?"

His eyes lit up and he said, "Oh, yes."

We were surprised, but began singing in harmony the beautiful words to this old song:

> That I am God, be still and know,
> Though storm-tossed be thy weary soul;
> Thy deepest grief to Him is woe,
> And over all He has control.

Be still and know, be still and know,
That He is God, be still and know;
He sees and feels thy deepest woe,
That He is God, be still and know;

Mr. Ali kept his eyes on us, listening intently. We continued:

Tho' shattered hopes surround thee still,
Tho' dark and rugged be thy way,
Know that for thee a Father's will
Doth order all things day by day.

Be still and know, be still and know,
That He is God, be still and know;
He sees and feels thy deepest woe,
That He is God, be still and know;

When we finished, he cried out, "I believe it. I believe every word of it. Thank you! Thank you!"

Ray asked "Would you like us to say a prayer for you?"

After we had prayed, he thanked us again and again. We said good night and left. The next Tuesday, Mr. Ali died. We expect to see him in the kingdom of heaven. Did he not believe all he was able? I think it corresponds to what Jesus said of Mary when she broke the alabaster box, "She hath done what she could."

The Hindu Holy Man

They shall take up serpents; and if they drink any deadly thing, it shall not hurt them.

Mark 16:18

Ray had not been practicing very long in Guyana when he had a Hindu Holy Man as a patient. As soon as Ray checked him over, the man said, "Now I must go visit your madam."

I heard the bell and went to the window to see who was there. One never opened the door without looking first. There he stood in his white baggy trousers with a tunic over them and a little incense lamp on a chain. He looked quite harmless so I let him in. We visited, then he asked to see my son. After that, he wanted something to drink.

Because of a dock strike in New York, our household goods did not arrive until after Christmas, about six months after we arrived. I had bought only a few dishes so had not much to offer my guest. I had no juice on hand and had to give him water. He seemed satisfied.

Every month he visited the doctor. Every month he always had to see "your madam." Each time he asked for a little more -- milk, then milk and bread, and so on until I was fixing him a full tray of food. Then we had some folk who had been missionaries in the far east and Asia came to attend a Guyana Conference and to hold a series of meetings for the church members. They ate breakfast with us (I borrowed dishes from the hospital). I told her about the visits from the Hindu Holy Man. She was noticeably perturbed.

"Don't you ever let him in again!" she said. "We had them where we were. We were warned about them. What he will do is this. He will keep asking for more and more: a little money then more money, etc. The day will come when you will not be able to give him what he asks. When you refuse, he will bring you a little sack of fruit for a gift. That fruit will be poisoned. Never, never let him in again."

When the meetings were over, the people left. One day Ray phoned to tell me the holy man was coming over. It was pouring rain. He said, "Now remember, you don't let him in. I know it will be hard, but don't let him in."

He came and knocked. He continued to knock. He had a large umbrella but it was raining so hard I could hardly stand not to open the door, but somehow I resisted. After many persistent knocks, he left.

When Ray came home for lunch, he carried a little paper bag. "Here is your poisoned fruit," he said. "The Hindu Holy Man came back after you didn't let him in and said, 'here is some fruit I want to give to your madam.'"

Many have asked if we had it tested. It never entered our minds to have this done. I suppose the evidence was too strong. How glad we were to have been warned! However, the promise of Mark 16:18 is just as applicable for fruit if the Lord so wills.

The Kitty Crusade

At that time Jesus answered and said, I thank thee, O Father, Lord of heaven and earth, because thou hast hid these things from the wise and prudent, and hast revealed them unto babes.

Matthew 11:25

Like all cities, Georgetown had many suburbs. One of these was called Kitty. We had our membership transferred from the USA to the Kitty Church. We were quite active in the church. I helped with cradle roll and kindergarten. Henry helped with the Primary division. There were a lot of children, even up to junior age and early teens. One day I counted forty children who were not children of members. They came in off the streets when they heard the singing. They enjoyed it so much that they returned week after week. They even stayed for the church services. For the most part, their parents had no religious affiliation.

We had a pastor and an assistant pastor. The assistant, *Pastor Morgan, was a young ministerial intern and very active. He enjoyed the children. Soon he and Henry became good friends. They and two young elders decided to hold a series of meetings in the Kitty district for those children and their parents. Such meetings were called crusades in Guyana. Much planning went into them. One thing needed was a place to meet. One of the mothers offered the use of her "bottom house". Because the city was below sea level, most houses were built six to eight feet from the ground on what we called "stilts". They were really pillars. This was to prevent flooding of the house during rainy season. The "bottom house" was the ground floor. It had a board floor with railing around it.

An old pump organ was found. Even though it was rather squeaky, Henry was able to play it as long as they selected the hymns he knew since he was mostly self-taught. There were no gimmicks, no videos, no professional music, no money — they had to make do with what they had. To help, they had special music by guests and Henry's trumpet. Since his was the only trumpet in the church in Guyana, it was always an attraction.

After one of the meetings, a car drove up to our house on the hospital compound. Henry came rushing in and said, "Daddy, come out to the car. Pastor Morgan needs you. He can't get out of the car." He was too excited to tell us more. We both ran out and were somehow able to get the pastor out of the car and into the hospital for X-rays. He had an injured back and bruises, but no broken bones.

Since Pastor Morgan had no car, he used a motorcycle and was on his way to the crusade at Kitty. The road was full of traffic; cars, motorcycles, bicycles, donkey carts, cows, goats and the inevitable taxi. The taxi drivers seemed to think everyone and everything must clear the way for them. One had stopped right in front of the pastor giving him no time to slow down or stop. Pastor Morgan was thrown up into the air where he turned a somersault and landed on his feet in front of the taxi.

As he turned the somersault, he prayed, "Lord, don't let me die. I've got to preach at Kitty tonight."

Dizzily he got up. Right there was a friend on a motorcycle. With no thought of his own motorcycle, Pastor Morgan hopped on behind the friend and said, "Please take me to Kitty. I've got to preach there tonight."

Amazingly, another friend was there to take care of the pastor's motorcycle. From Henry, we heard what went on at Kitty. The song leader had kept the song service going, expecting the pastor any time. He did not want the people to leave. Henry kept pumping and playing the old organ until he had played all the hymns he knew. They were about to close with prayer when the pastor showed up, limping to the platform. With no preliminaries, he said, "Good evening friends. Satan did not want me to preach here tonight and he almost took my life, but I'm here anyway. There must be someone here that Jesus wants to hear this sermon, someone who will yield to Jesus tonight."

And there was. It was Elizabeth's first time at the meeting. She was young, wild and living a sinful life. As she listened to the sermon, she said to herself, "I am the one. Pastor's life was saved for me to hear this message."

At the closing altar call, Elizabeth came forward. Soon she was baptized. Not long after, she came to visit Pastor Morgan. Her mother was going into the interior near the Brazil border and Elizabeth felt she should go along. The pastor tried to discourage her. It was a rough settlement with much drinking and dancing. She would be lonely and he feared she might go back to her former lifestyle.

Elizabeth insisted. She said, "No Pastor. I will teach them about Jesus."

She went. It was six miles from the Brazil border, no real roads - just rough trails, gas trucks once a month and not many people. About six weeks later, Pastor Morgan received a letter from her. In typical creolese, she wrote, "Pastor, I go' six soul for baptize. Please come for baptize. Please send worker for teach 'em." She also told her story. She and five more, one of them a little eight-year-old girl, went for a drive to the Brazil border in a jeep. On the way home, the jeep ran out of gas. There was no gas for miles and miles. The gas truck was not due for two weeks. While debating what to do, Elizabeth said, "We can pray."

Everyone except the little girl laughed and mocked her, but Elizabeth and the little girl knelt beside the jeep and Elizabeth began to pray. The others, not knowing what to do, also knelt. Elizabeth prayed a simple prayer. When she got up from her knees, she said, "Now, I go for walk. I go for find gas." She believed we should do all we can to answer our own prayers.

There was more laughing and mocking but Elizabeth and the little girl started toward home to find gas. Before they got very far they heard shouting behind them. They were being called back. There by the jeep was a gas truck. After the jeep was filled and the gas truck left, Elizabeth and the girl fell upon their knees in gratitude to the Lord for answered prayer. The others knelt, too. This time there was no laughing and no mocking. Now they questioned Elizabeth regarding her faith. She explained it all and before they reached home, all had accepted Christ. That was five souls. What about the sixth one?

When she arrived home, Elizabeth shared the story with her mother who was so impressed that she also yielded her heart to Jesus. Elizabeth then held more studies with them and now wrote for the pastor to come to baptize them.

Permanent Return

My God shall supply all your need according to his riches in glory by Christ Jesus.

Philippians 4:19

By 1978, Ray was having a series of obstructions, eating little and losing energy. We asked for a vacation thinking this would help. It did not. We decided against returning to the mission field. A short time later Ray had to be hospitalized and was diagnosed as having advanced Crohn's disease, the result of the contamination during his first surgery. Not being able to practice medicine, he applied for disability and I went to work at a local hospital.

Although we had signed a waiver stating that we would not claim sustentation after retiring, due to the circumstances the committee kindly voted us full sustentation. This included a monthly check with medical and other benefits according to policy. Now we were not entitled to disability money from the church. But our trust was in the Lord who has promised to provide. This time, unknown to us, He worked through Ray's brother. Don met with the committee and reminded them of the medical error in diagnosis that was responsible for our present condition. He also reminded them of the workload Ray had to carry while in Guyana. The committee voted to give us full sustentation. This included a monthly check, medical payments and other benefits in keeping with their policy for returned missionaries.

These benefits continue. With so much home nursing care for Ray, at age 62 I decided to retire. The doctor allowed me to do some things at home that helped avoid many a stay in the hospital, but about 1982, the obstruction had to be removed again. This time it was from adhesions and there was no sign of Crohn's disease. The Lord had healed it.

In 1988, Ray obstructed again from adhesions. The surgeon said, "There is no sign of Crohn's disease, so he never had it." He insisted that once you have Crohn's, it does not heal. However, we had a copy of the pathology report and the verification of many well-qualified physicians that it was Crohn's. All I can say is that we have something the surgeon does not have - a belief in a God who heals.

It has been many years since that surgery. Previously Ray was on a very restrictive diet. Now he is able to eat most foods. He will never regain his lost strength but we are content and give thanks to our heavenly Father for His constant watchcare. We can truly say with the Psalmist *"The Lord is the portion of mine inheritance and of my cup; thou maintainest my lot. The lines are fallen unto me in pleasant places; yea, I have a goodly heritage. I will bless the Lord"* Psalm 16:5-7.

Mission Offerings

The children of Israel brought a willing offering unto the Lord, every man and woman, whose heart made them willing.

Exodus 35:29

Before going into mission service, I worked with children in Sabbath School and Vacation Bible School. In Sabbath School, we always took up a mission offering. I would give each child an interesting container to take home. I asked them to give up soda drinks and candy to put money into the container. At the end of three months, the offering went to a mission project. Each quarter, it went to a different part of the world. Before we went as missionaries, there was a special offering to Linda Vista College in Mexico to help finish the girl's dorm. What a thrill it was for me to one day go as a missionary and give a talk in the parlor of that very dorm! This happened soon after we arrived at Yerba Buena and I was invited to come to Linda Vista which was only a five minute run down the hill from us.

From Sabbath School we also sent money to help build the Davis Memorial Hospital in South America. At the time, the name meant nothing to me. I did not dream that one day I would be walking the halls of that hospital, teaching practical nurses, making patient rounds with my husband and singing with him for the patients. While serving there, I often thought of the little children who helped to build it.

Chapter 11

Conclusion

Time goes on. It is now 2005 as the second edition of this book appears. We had our golden wedding anniversary in 1996. We are getting older and more feeble, yet each time I take my memory pictures down and recall how God has directed our paths, I am amazed. I have come to realize that God's care need not be outstanding as in the many experiences of my life. He does that for some but He has taught me another lesson. The common, everyday provision of our daily needs is even more wonderful. How is it that every month our checks arrive? How is it that I can go shopping every week and bring home beautiful fruits and vegetables? How is it that through these years, we have never lacked, that we can wash our clothes, that we have loving children?

It all seems so routine, and yet, "in him we live, and move, and have our being." Acts 17:28. Is it not outstanding that breath follows breath? Heartbeat follows heartbeat? It was hard to accept the fact that we could not go back to our dear friends in Guyana, but I have learned that we can serve God right where we are. He is pleased when we do our best wherever we are when we do it by faith in the atoning blood of Jesus.

In all my ways Thy hand I own,
Thy ruling providence I see;
Assist me still my course to run,
And still direct my paths to Thee.

Still hath my life new wonders seen
Repeated every year:
Behold, my days which yet remain
I trust them to thy care.

— Charles Wesley

I pray that God will bless this little book to the encouragement of many souls in the upward way and that He will "direct your paths."

Ray passed away Oct. 2006.

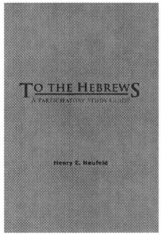

CPSIA information can be obtained at www.ICGtesting.com
Printed in the USA
270242BV00002B/39/A